PLACITIS INFECTAS

Surviving
Elitism
Handbook

R.A. Roth

I0437014

outskirts
press

Surviving Elitism Handbook
All Rights Reserved.
Copyright © 2017 R. A. Roth
v1.0

The opinions expressed in this manuscript are solely the opinions of the author and do not represent the opinions or thoughts of the publisher. The author has represented and warranted full ownership and/or legal right to publish all the materials in this book.

This book may not be reproduced, transmitted, or stored in whole or in part by any means, including graphic, electronic, or mechanical without the express written consent of the publisher except in the case of brief quotations embodied in critical articles and reviews.

Outskirts Press, Inc.
http://www.outskirtspress.com

ISBN: 978-1-4787-8896-6

Cover Photo © 2017 R. A. Roth. All rights reserved - used with permission.

Outskirts Press and the "OP" logo are trademarks belonging to Outskirts Press, Inc.

PRINTED IN THE UNITED STATES OF AMERICA

Table of Contents

III: Surviving Elitism

IV: Surviving Elitism

Introduction

Do you believe you are a reasonably intelligent person? Most folks do. I'm sure you think for yourself, and certainly would never tolerate being manipulated or influenced into believing something that is not true or at least somewhat inaccurate.

I am also convinced that you would never entertain damaging your country in any way, nor obstructing efforts to improve the problems that we face in today's changing world; in particular the ever growing cultural societal division that has found its way into all of our lives. ...And, done just to protect your ideologies and opinions.

It would be difficult to imagine that there are those who actually set themselves above these concerns; doing it for nothing more than to enhance their own position, coupled with an innate necessity to be and remain in control. Those people are convinced that their ideological and opinionated agenda is the only correct perception of how the world around us is governed. They demand the need to be recognized as superior; they are *elitists*.

I: Surviving Elitistism

I - 1

The Concern

BEFORE I GET started on my rant, I want to make sure you do not misunderstand my commentary. I comprehend the meaning of elite, and fully understand that there are those who are part of an elite group within any aspect of any society. Most importantly they, deservedly, reside in an elite status due to their talent, character, or wealth, which has elevated them to that elite class.

This document will center on those, who may or may not contain the above attributes in varying degrees, but those who egotistically perceive themselves as being an elite; an arrogance in believing they are, in fact, *superior* to others. I will be speaking about those who are *elitists,* who practice knowingly or not, *elitism.* My goal is to highlight the damage that this type of individual or group of individuals can do, and have already done to our society.

Elitism is not a new concern by any means. The elitist has been with us forever. So, why now is it becoming a paramount issue in our society and culture of today? Well, if I were to answer that with any specificity, I probably would come off as being an elitist. I can offer, as an opinion, that the sciences of communication from our personal ability to communicate to any and all aspects of the media certainly has had an impact. We are bombarded with input on every aspect of life, love and the pursuit of happiness, with no real filter on what is real and what is not. The byproduct of this is when an individual or group bubbles up to some level of recognition within our hyper-communicative lifestyle; they immediately gain, to some degree, national distinction and credibility.

In many cases, this credibility probably has nothing to do with intellect or innate abilities, and on its own is a real *"so what."* But, it does give a platform to many, who never or ever could have had such an opportunity to present their *opinions* to literally millions.

This is where the danger of an elitist behavior comes in; *"opinions."* Yes, we all have opinions, and yes, we all know what opinions are like... We are a people of opinions; which in its own way is wonderful, and all opinions illustrated by any reasonable person, in any civilized society, should find some level of respect.

But, before we go too far let's make sure we fully understand what an opinion is:

"A view or judgment formed about something, not necessarily based on fact or knowledge."

This is where the elitist, in our society, steps in. They have opinions, and they know, unequivocally, that *their* opinions and *their* rational is far superior to others. That's great! Good for them. But now, take that individual or group, give them a platform, let them state and share their opinions as fact; as a reality; although it is not; then given their particular position, charisma and level of notoriety, blended with a powerful ego and you have yourself an elitist.

The point here is opinions are nothing more than *opinions*, they are not fact. If they are based on fact and resolvable as a fact, they are no longer an opinion, they are in fact, *fact*. I know we could argue this statement, but at least give me this, one plus one is two, that is a fact, it is provable and reliable. If a fact cannot be held to that standard, and is not factually verifiable, it is an opinion. The ego driven elitist will assure you that their opinion is fact, and do it in a very convincing way. *Beware...*

I - 2

Identification

LET'S FACE IT, being called, or at least being perceived as an elitist portrays an arrogant personality, and an insulting characterization of anyone. Yet, somehow those who display such disturbing behavior seem to be growing in number, although I doubt any of this growing, self-appointed horde see themselves as practicing elitism. They just somehow know that they are right about virtually everything, while the rest of us; the pathetic hoi polli, have no idea what is good for ourselves, and must be directed and controlled by their far superior intellect and knowledge.

Now, before we go any farther, let us make sure we fully understand what being an elitist entails:

"The attitude or behavior of a person, or group who regard themselves as belonging to a privileged level of class or society."

"The belief that certain persons, or members of certain groups deserve favored treatment by virtue of their superiority; as in intelligence, social standing, or wealth."

Do I believe there are those who are intellectually superior to others, or that there are those who hold a significant financial rank in wealth? Of course I do, although as for the "social standing" aspect of elitism, *not so much*. I believe that is just a byproduct of the other two, although let's face it, there seems to be a growing set of those self-anointed social superiors.

With that said the question then is: Do these supposed intellectually superior, or the above average holders of wealth deserve to direct, control, preach to, or judge the rest of the less intelligent and/or wealthy?

This question is easy to answer; ***of course not!***

But, how can I possibly say that? Did I not just state there are those who are intellectually and/or financially superior? That is where the problem comes in... Those attributes, alone, fall far short of truly elevating anyone to a position in which they become part of a privileged ruling class. For that matter no one individual or group should ever distinguish themselves as being superior to the populous.

Those who are given the capacity for knowledge and understanding should fully comprehend that by *believing they* are *superior* to others now makes them an elitist, displaying the arrogance of a self-appointed elite.

What factors determine one's intellect; family background; level of education; intelligence quotient, or the ability to convince others that they just know better? I guess the easy answer is all of the above, but none of us are just a product of pure intellect.

We are formed and governed by innate abilities (genetics) and nurturing (environment,) and regardless of our supposed intelligence we also carry formed opinions and ideologies. One could argue that based on this heightened level of intellect, one's formed opinions and ideologies would be quite sound and correct; that they are now infallible in their knowledge and judgment. To date, I doubt throughout all of history, anyone could name a single individual who could claim infallibility.

Yet, we have individuals and groups who regularly point out how "stupid" millions of people are, and do it with no qualms; because they know better. Their ideologies and opinions are far superior, and the rest of us must understand that *fact*.

How can one identify an elitist? Well, there are numerous signs that can be observed, starting with an elitist *never* admits to being wrong or mistaken in any of their actions, opinions or facts. Often their ability to spin their opinions into fact is astounding. They cherry pick bits and pieces of various real facts, which are then extrapolated into what they now believe is a single supportable reality; making their *opinion* a "fact."

They rarely, if ever, admit to their own failings, even when provided with proof positive. They will point to and blame virtually everyone and everything else to explain how their opinions and actions are not the problem, it is always someone else. In many cases their efforts of denial reach astounding levels, and are perfectly willing to promote damage to our country to prove it. This is done both politically and culturally, all to protect their opinionated correctness. Ultimately, like a petulant child, they will display frustration and anger, and done with a tantrum like behavior. If things do not go their way, *plan on conflict.*

The elitist is no stranger to hypocrisy. It is amazing on how often they will state an opinion, which typically highlights the *stupidity* of those who are not as informed and knowledgeable as they are. Although, when that very opinion now no longer substantiates or has somehow reversed their position on any given subject, they will refute any ownership to their previous comments or actions. Even when confronted with the realities of their stated opinions, they will once again prove to be quite practiced at talking their way out by using some form of convoluted denial or external blame. They are never the problem, it is always someone else.

The elitist becomes most vicious when they are ignored and rejected. This is where their true hypocrisy is displayed. They are truly masterful at diminishing those who they deem substandard to themselves. They will resort to name calling, insults and belittling of massive groups of individuals who do not have the public recognition, or access to a platform permitting a response to those attacks. If this behavior were to take place from those who they are now attacking, they would not hesitate to demonize those actions; even going as far as publicly calling them deplorable, and attempting to delegitimize their position.

One would think that we could easily see and then reject such an individual; sadly this is not the case. There are areas of this country which draw and nurture the elitist mentality; like-minds that find their way to believing they know better than the rest of us who do not share their opinions.

One thing that must always be remembered about the elitist, they typically live in a supportive bubble, which protects them from understanding others who do not, or cannot, live their life-style, and to benefit from the positions that they enjoy. Rather than trickledown economics, these select areas practice trickle down elitism; where elitist ideologies and opinions become in-cestuous within their realm of existence. Anything outside of their opinion must be attacked, insulted and completely dimin-ished. Tolerance is not one of their attributes.

In reality, the elitist has no desire to live the life that they preach for the rest of us. They know what is best for us, but they will not be living by those sermonized opinions; that would be far below their position. This behavior is clearly hypocritical. One thing the elitist will champion is tolerance, using it as a rally cry to their principled world of existence, until they are opposed in any way. They then become the most intolerant individual or group imaginable and done with no self-awareness of their hypocrisy.

We are all elitists in our own way. Our ideologies, formed over years, limits our span of tolerance of others' thoughts and opinions. So, we tend to see those who do not agree with us as less knowledgeable.

Now, although I state that these ideologies are formed over years, in reality the major portion of our beliefs are formed at a young age. Our parents and childhood environment delineates what our adult thoughts and opinions ultimately become. These lessons of life learned during our impres-sionable years are acquired through our innate ability to comprehend the reality of the world around us. We have had

Presidents, in their own writings, discuss how important their father has been in formulating their ideological view of how the country should be governed. Maybe that's good, and then again, *maybe not.*

So, we all carry the elitist gene *(so to speak)* in varying degrees; part of human nature I guess. No one likes to be wrong, and admitting to being wrong can be, for some, quite painful, and felt as being personally demeaning. We all want to be seen as being knowledgeable, we all struggle for respect, and we all certainly have opinions. But, that level of an elitist's attitude is not what we are discussing.

We are looking at those who have found their way to having input to the populous, a bully pulpit; a position of perceived power. We can admit to some degree that their intellect, education, wealth, and ego have brought them to this level of recognition. But, they have also brought with them opinions and ideologies, whether right or wrong, that governs who they are; regardless of real or perceived intelligence. The years of internally compartmentalizing, legitimizing, and developing a pampered self-indulgent personality permeates every thought and opinion. This now entitles them to enjoy a privileged class of existence, and well above the rest of us.

Who are these elitists? Well, I assume they have been around since the beginning of time. There always seems to be someone who wants to tell us what we are doing wrong, with their opinions being the only answer. They have been the rulers of the world, some tyrants, some generous, some brilliant, and some with no concept of what they are doing at all. But, they all shared one thing, they knew more than the rest of us.

I - 3

Where Are They?

HOW DOES THE elitist practice their trade? As mentioned earlier, even though we may all have a bit of that behavior in us, elitism truly raises its ugly head when coupled with a super-ego. I speak of those who are dedicated to being in the public eye, needing to gain the adulation and admiration of the masses, and to literally be recognized as being superior. They will pursue status that provides them with a much sought after exposure, and are terribly desperate to gain influence.

For those who find themselves in a position of public recognition or visibility; such as politics, academia, journalism, entertainment, or any individual or group that has ascertained a level of public recognition are now part of the supposed elite class.

By the way, none of those above mentioned positions requires a great amount of intellect to find their way to their various positions. Sure, a reasonable amount of intellect is required for virtually any position, but the level of intelligence rarely encompasses every aspect of human ability and existence.

Let us take a look at the individual professions that seems to draw the elitist mentality...

I - 4

Academia

THIS SHOULD GO without saying, but no school, at any level, funded in any form by the government *(the people,)* must ever permit, nor endorse any teacher, professor, counselor, principal, superintendent, school board, or any agent of that school or school system, indoctrinating personal ideologies or opinions. And, for those who find that comment contrary to the First Amendment, please take a moment to think about it.

Do you really want any educator preaching their personal philosophies to your children, while it is our government *(your money)* funding that unsolicited opinion based commentary? Yes, you can inspire conversation and debate about subjects, but they must be conducted in a totally unbiased environment. Most importantly, the educator must stick to the subject, if you teach math, *teach math*; and if you teach social science, teach it as a science and not as a platform for your ideological opinions.

When I talk about academia I am referring to a college level education, and specifically the private institutions. This group in particular can be quite dangerous; knowledge of any particular subject has little to do with ideological opinions, and yet this is what many of the academic community uses as fact.

Of course their supposed superior position mandates, within themselves, that they share their ideological beliefs as reality.

The true danger from academia is often plainly displayed in classroom behavior, which in many cases reeks of attempts at social engineering. Within the past years, a growing front of self-appointed keepers of the truth have found their way to some notoriety by their inability to control their ideologically opinionated classroom rants. In many cases they totally fail to accept any other opinion, and have reflected this in the actual grading of a dissenting student.

This behavior has escalated to such an extreme that insulting, belittling, and humiliation is sometimes used to enforce their beliefs. Many of these extremely idealistic educators are living within a bubble of like-minded individuals. Their view outside of that bubble is limited, and carries with it an elitist arrogance which supports their opinions; with no regard for reality or the thoughts and needs of others having differing opinions and ideologies.

Once again, the true hypocrisy of the elitist is displayed. If there is any place that should teach and promote tolerance it *must* be in this environment of academic enlightenment. Openness of opinions and ideas must be honored and respected, rather than limiting speech through the use of such asinine concepts as a *"safe space,"* and/or through ridicule and exclusion of those with differing opinions. It is genuine bigoted censorship in every respect, and done by those who should legitimately know better.

The level of intolerance displayed in many of our universities today is embarrassing at best, and most likely socially and culturally damaging. It promotes segregation and exclusionary behavior. The arrogance of many university educators by promoting a closed minded society, which demonizes anyone with a contrary opinion, is astonishing.

The level of elitism in our college institutions is at a critical level. You can have your opinions, but not at the expense of others, and certainly not by the use of censorship. Many of the universities today have turned into promoters of bigotry, and done by the elitists now in a position of authority.

If you do not share their narrow and exclusionary vision, you will be ridiculed, and most likely branded with demeaning names ranging from racist to Nazi, done with nothing more than their ability to add ignorance to arrogance. Sadly, far too many of the students fail to see this growing attack on tolerance, permitting their thoughts and opinions to be socially engineered to conform to an uninformed, intolerant, bigoted, elitist academic institution.

I - 5

News Media/Journalism

IT IS A tossup between academia and journalism as it relates to displaying arrogant elitist behavior. I guess the question would be what came first; the sheltered intolerant opinionated education, or the biased, selective news media reporting process?

What has influenced the other to become this cultural embarrassment of bigotry? What should be, as a rule, the purest, unbiased and most trusted of professions has degraded into an elitist love fest of like opinions, far removed from reporting real news. It has reached such a degree of bias they no longer make any attempt at cloaking this atrocious behavior.

For the most part the news you receive has been selectively filtered to insure that you do not hear all the *real* reportable news that does not fit their agenda. In recent years the news media/journalism has stepped up their attack on differing opinions by literally banning news which does not support their preconceived ideologies.

This comes from the media centers of the country, which feeds on their own opinions, but displays an unbelievable ignorance about the country as a whole. In today's world they will go out of their way to insult and demean those living outside of their protected bubble of existence, pointing out how millions of our population are ignorant, uneducated and really have no right to their own opinions or ideologies. The all-knowing, well-educated journalists *know* better.

Along with their lack of reporting on all the news, they have also taken on the manufacturing of news. Within the past decade, the number of false, misleading, biased and flat out fake editorials that masquerade as real news reporting has become a mainstay, and coming from what should be a respected and trusted news media source.

This aspect of our society has reached such a point of mistrust that its relevance is quickly diminishing. Opinions must never influence what and how news is reported. The elitist is so entrenched in their own little world, and so confident they are *always* right, they will, without hesitation, manipulate, deceive, ignore, deny and manufacture news needed to support their ideology.

We live in a time when the news media now feels empowered to socially engineer this country with their ideals, and does so quite openly with an arrogant elitist superiority.

It is interesting to see where this concentration of such single minded opinions and behavior comes from. Media centers of this country tend to conflate their sheltered beliefs into thinking the entire country must share their opinions and ideologies. This will be accomplished by any means necessary, and since they do have the position of power, at least from direct access to reporting news to the rest of the country, they can interject their opinions and beliefs as reality.

I certainly support opinion editorial pieces as long as they are identified as such, but when news reporting is corrupted by ideologies, we all become prisoners of their beliefs, and are left with false narratives. Those living within this intolerant environment feel superior to others since they hold the information authority.

Once again, we see the elitist behavior, which inevitably displays levels of intolerance that is so contrary to what these individuals should be supporting.

They typically talk down to those who differ or oppose their opinions, by mentioning what they see as ignorant at best, but for the most describe as just plain *stupid*. When confronted with facts or specific information proving them to be inaccurate or biased, you will see them laugh with a smug, dismissive demeanor, then deny and typically deflect the subject matter with a righteous air of superiority.

Some issues they have manipulated are outrageous in concept, yet because of the source; believable to many in this country who are far too uninformed to realize it. The news media is quite confident that their opinionated commentary should be the law of the land.

Combating these elitists is virtually impossible. Sadly, their need to be superior, their need for exposure, notoriety, and being the spokesperson for humanity is so deep-seated, that I doubt that real news will ever find its way back to a trusted position.

Today's journalistic reporting is aligned with their self-perceived flawless ideologies, and supported by the academic social engineer that is in the process of developing the next generation of intolerant elitists. This again perpetuates their bubble of social existence; divorced from understanding the country they contend to report on. I recognize the complexities of youthful questioning of the status quo, but at some point the realities of their own intolerance for opposing opinions must be recognized.

The elitist personality is incapable of seeing anything but their opinions. Such a misappropriation of this position of trust will ultimately divide our country, and in fact, over the past decade, has to a considerable degree already done so.

I - 6

Entertainment

THE ENTERTAINMENT INDUSTRY is rich with elitism; fostered by their public exposure and recognition.

One must first understand the mentality of these individuals; their very profession delineates the need to be seen, to be important, and to be typically believed as the characters they portray. Their egos are so powerful that they have lost their way to the realities of our country. They speak to us as if we are children at best, and more likely just plain stupid, and done so as if they are the only ones who can fully comprehend right from wrong. They tend to be shameless in their rants and insults when their concepts of how the world should be are challenged.

They will threaten to leave the country if things do not go their way, but they never do. Childish comments are repeatedly stated, and said with a supposed altruistic ideology, which in truth has little basis in reality. For the most part they are looking for attention, their need to be noticed, and a need for adulation from the masses will motivate them more than any cause they may champion.

They play to their audience with virtually no consideration

provided to the country's benefit. They lose their credibility when they start the name calling and the insulting of millions of Americans. They are so arrogant they literally believe they have some type of power, which of course they do not. They live in a make believe world of importance; with nothing more than a belief in their own bullshit. *Elitism at its finest!*

Now, do not get me wrong, they certainly have a right to their opinions and ideologies. Let's face it, their opinions are just that, their opinions, with no more validity than yours or mine. Their ego and need to be important displays a desperate need to be influential, and done to the point of true embarrassment. They, of course, do not see that within themselves. They are convinced of this because they are *entertainers*, recognized by millions, which somehow makes them superior to the millions they talk down to.

They are continually provided with platforms to air, unfiltered, their opinions and beliefs, from nationally broadcast award shows, to self-authored displays, which find their way to national attention.

Their confidence in their sheltered world of ideologies knows no bounds. They exhibit egos so outrageous in presentation it is hard to comprehend, let alone watch. Their rhetoric has become so insulting to the millions that they openly diminish, it is amazing that it is not recognized and reported on by the news media. Now, the news media does report on them, but their narratives are used to support the intolerant bigoted attack on the populous.

Sadly, our entertainment industry, in general, has become a

center for elitism; once again, supported through the incestuous relationship of the closed society they reside in. With the
exception of just a few specific, highly populated urban centers, they have little idea of what life is like for the remainder
of this country. Their behavior appears to display a care less
attitude; they are superior to you, and far more intelligent. If
you do not believe me, just ask them, they will gladly confirm
my assumption.

Now one would think, what does it matter what a bunch of
entertainers think or believe? Well, it shouldn't, but along
with the intolerant self-centered elitists of the news media,
and the current self-indulgent biases of academia, this country is in trouble.

I - 7

Politics

POLITICS IS ULTIMATELY where the rubber meets the road. All the egos, opinions, ideologies, jealousies, deceptions and manipulations converge, and at the top of this pile of self-centered behavior is the elitist politician. In reality, it is not the country that is at the forefront of their concerns, but rather it is their need to promote and put into place their ideology, and most importantly to stay in office.

The elitist has a mission, and it is a single minded one. It is their vision of the world, and as altruistic as it may sound, or in fact be; in the end it will fall far short of its goal. This presents an image that does not provide a concern for the entire country, but rather just select groups or policies. However, ultimately, it is all about them.

It does not matter how these select groups may require intervention, there must be a balance in caring, which serves all the citizens of this country. For the most part that is not the way politics works.

Promises are made to help specific groups of the population, for one reason only, and that is: **votes!** To use a quote from TV show House of Cards: "Generosity is its' own form of control." Now, it is a rarity that these promises are ever kept, but if they are, they will be at the expense of others. Taking from one to give to another has become commonplace in our country today. Any opposition to this will typically find that opponent being demonized and ridiculed.

Attempts at demonizing and diminishing half the country in the name of supporting a single minded, ego driven ideology is so outrageous that it seems ridiculous in just saying it. Yet, elitists of today seemly give little regard to the damage they are doing to this country, it inevitably is about them, and their opinions. In their eyes there is no room for negotiation or compromise, which is continually displayed in words and actions.

The current philosophy of dividing the country whether by race, income, education or beliefs has been in past years rather successful. A country divided is a country easily manipulated. A country divided is ripe for social engineering, and the ego driven elitist politician possessing a solely ideologically formulated strategy is more than willing to step into that role.

A successful elitist politician is characteristically well educated with excellent presentation skills and usually very charismatic. Certainly, all wonderful attributes, and that description could, possibly, also describe a successful non-elitist politician. So, how does one separate one from the other? Well, to paraphrase *Nancy Pelosi;* you have to put them in office to see what they can do. Sadly, not good way to proceed with any aspect of political decisions, but the options are few.

You could research and review their background and previous activities. But, it will be a difficult task. The information you find will tend to be scrubbed by the media in such a way that finding the full story will be difficult. Plus, keep in mind that the individual you are reviewing probably would not be running for office if their background could not stand reasonable scrutiny. True levels of vetting of a candidate by the news media is generally skewed in the direction of the journalist's biased opinion. So, you take a flier and put this seeming wonderful individual in whatever office they seek.

From that point on, determining their elitist tendencies is easy. Within a reasonable amount of time in office have they failed to keep major campaign promises? Do they appear to defend special interest groups or segments of the population rather than all the people? Are they openly dismissive and insulting to any opposition concerning their policies? Do they deflect compromise and negotiations? Are they exclusive rather than inclusive in their decision making? Do they fail at being transparent in their activities? Do they manipulate the media? Do they refuse to change a position, policy, or display any flexibility in opinion; even though it is obvious their policies and opinions are going in the wrong direction? Do they micromanage cultural social issues? Do they openly demonize certain opposing individuals? Do they refuse to take responsibility for their failed actions and policies?

The ideologically motivated politician is most identified by their inability to change direction when their opinionated strategies prove to be failing. Back-tracking on their unsuccessful, if not disastrous policies will never happen. Admitting to any failure is not part of their temperament; they are never wrong.

Now, the elitist press media will never draw attention to this, in fact they will supply cover by typically placing the blame for these breakdowns on others. Interestingly enough, when the opposition displays the ability to change direction on any policy, because it *is* the right thing to do, the elitist media will immediately criticize this action with terms such as "flip-flopping," "indecisive," and of course the ever famous "chaotic" situation.

All, or some of the above actions point to an elitist's behavior. Now, let's make sure we understand that all politicians have egos, big ones at that. So, an ego driven *elitist* politician is what we are discussing. The concern is regardless of how intelligent, polished, diplomatic, or charismatic this individual is, they are not concerned with all of us, just those they can get to support and believe in them.

Remember this individual is very confident with their ideology, opinions and feelings on what motivates them. It is not the betterment of all, just a targeted constituency. They have a vision, and if that vision is the restructuring of our society, both politically and culturally, we are in for *trouble*.

I - 8

The Followers

LET ME OPEN with some advice as it relates to family and friends who display an elitist behavior...

We all have at least a couple of folks in our life that somehow have it in their head they know it all. Arguing or discussing an issue with these individuals is fruitless, nothing will be achieved. They will not be swayed by facts or evidence, they will always be right, and nothing is going to change their mind.

So I offer a line from a letter written, April 22, 1800, to William Hamilton, from Thomas Jefferson who wrote:

"I never considered a difference of opinion in politics, in religion, in philosophy, as cause for withdrawing from a friend."

These words offer the start to putting this country back together. Once the self-involved elitist politician is removed from the formula, compromise and understanding can, and will, come to the forefront.

Are we civilized enough to come together? I doubt it, but let us at least set aside the extreme acrimony; all it does is promote division, and an exclusionary behavior that accomplishes nothing.

Opinions can be quite valid, and when dealing with a reasonably rational individual there is no reason you cannot listen and respect their opinions; they in turn should be able to listen to yours. Stay clear, or at least be guarded of those who are so close-minded they would rather not associate with you than listen to something that may be fact, but goes against their rigid elitist ideology. Remember they are always right; these folks are very easy to spot.

The elitist survives by the use of position, influence, charisma and manipulation. Those who support and follow the *opinions* of the elitist determines the level of power the elitist controls. Now, please note, I mentioned opinions, not facts.

Yes, the elitist will give lip service to real issues, but rarely will they ever be seriously addressed. The elitist's survival depends upon opinions which are rather lofty, global, and altruistic, which in an untroubled, truly civilized world would justify a worthwhile pursuit.

The elitist's failure to deal with or even face the realities that surround them is found within their fear of failure. If issues in our country are so obvious and pronounced that it is corroding our way of life; putting the future of the nation at risk, you would think it should be on the top of the to-do list for any politician to tackle and resolve. Yet, these issues continue unresolved, year after year, and in most cases diminished in importance, if not totally ignored. *Why?*

Once in power the elitist personality will minimize these issues because they dread the thought of failure in resolving what should be resolvable, or at least genuinely addressed. In many cases they will actually aggravate these serious social and national security issues, then using targeted commentary places blame on a specific individual, group, or often a major portion of the population. Typically, the well positioned news media will support these actions, because they certainly would not want to be found lacking in true concern for our global initiatives, so the lofty ideals will win out.

Now, we have those who support this behavior, they are the believers in promises that are never kept, embracing the charismatic elitist who embraces failed diplomacy over action, and deception over transparence.

The elitist, lemming-like follower falls within two obvious categories. The first is the supposed *informed individual*; now I say "supposed" because they characteristically only pay attention to what they want to hear. Their ability to take notice of anything outside of their closed ideological realm is very limited, if not non-existent. Facts that are contrary to their opinions are brushed off as false, and for every argument opposing their opinion, regardless of merit, is met with a smug condescendence. They never let facts, or reality for that matter, get in the way of their all-knowing ideology.

The second category is the uninformed *(of course!,)* they have no idea what is going on, but they are very passionate about it. These are the folks on the frontlines for elitist. They are the most motivated, feeding off of misleading headlines, buzz-phrases, talking head comedians, movie star rhetoric, or best of all their like-minded *"informed"* friends. They easily align with the altruistic vision presented by the captivating elitist persona. Most importantly, they are easily manipulated.

This group is also the most likely to be the protester in the street, and when interviewed they rarely have a coherent explanation on why they are protesting. Often these protests involve vandalism, property damage and attacks on anyone displaying opposition to their opinionated concepts; all done with no regard to the harm they cause to individuals, the community, and to our entire country.

These elitist supporters represent the epitome of intolerance and bigotry. All they know is that the opinions and ideologies, which they maintain, are the only true and correct concepts. They cannot comprehend why everyone does not see things as they do, and refuse to listen to any opposing or differing views.

As the elitist attacks the opposition with accusations, typically framed with their favorite indictments such as "racist," or "Nazi," the followers amplify this message, embracing every comment as the holy grail of righteousness, giving them license to carry out any action regardless of the damage it may do. Thus, the opposition is demonized, the media has its' story, and the elitist has its' assemblage

The elitist, by nature, will attack any opposition to their opinions, using the most demeaning, divisive, and demonizing methods possible. These diatribes are applauded by their followers, who see these verbal attacks as marching orders entitling them to act out in any fashion. These actions are typically destructive to the public in general, with no regard for the turmoil being caused.

Now, let me make this clear, before I'm accused of being against a lawful protest. I am not. But, I am against any protest based solely on a desire to cause disorder, chaos, anarchy, and most typically to promote *hate*. I am particularly adverse to paid for protesters, characteristically financed by political operatives. Meanwhile, the media covers this mayhem as if it was caused by the opposition to the elitist's tantrum, and successfully manipulating their followers.

Before we leave our discussion on the elitist supporters, let us just take a look at the personality of that supporter. They tend to be major elitists in their own right; they are rather self-centered and in many cases display a certain degree of narcissism. They rarely admit to not knowing something, typically they know everything. If they are a family member or friend, you will note that they rarely, if ever, pay you a complement, or acknowledge that you really know anything, and whatever they own it is always superior to what you own.

When it comes to discussing any subject it usually becomes a competition, with them always knowing more. They are happy to point out flaws in anything you have, or have done, and typically done in a passive aggressive way. On the surface one might say it is a form a jealousy, but it is not. They just know they are superior to you, and they cannot help themselves in making that point clear.

This is not to say they are not good, loving people, I am sure they are. This is a side of their personality, they are who they are. They are not capable of identifying these traits within themselves, and whether it is your mother, father, sister, brother, friend or neighbor they are protecting what, in many cases, is a delicate persona.

There is an innate fear of intellectual inadequacy, and certainly for the most part an unwarranted anxiety or concern. They have picked a lane in life, and they will not change. No fact or presentation will ever change their guarded outlook. In reality we all suffer to varying degrees this very condition. Whether misguided or right on the money, we all protect our opinions and ideological beliefs.

I do urge all of us to do one thing, please do not opt to *celebrate* the failures of your opponent when your opinion based hatred has seemingly been proven right. What is more important, your *opinion* being confirmed, or damage to the country? Displays of joy with smug satisfaction; done at the expense of this country moving forward, is a sad commentary on your true concern for all citizens.

I - 9

Free Speech

WE NOW LIVE an era where free speech is under attack, and attacked by the very people who are, or should be, constantly promoting it. The new philosophy is: the only freedom of speech that is permitted is the speech that agrees with the elitist's ideologies. Anything else must be dismissed, shouted down, and stopped by using any means necessary. What has always amazed me is why such an effort is made to shield the public from differing points of view? Is that not what this country was founded upon? The arrogance of the opinionated elitist, and those who support such behavior, certainly knows no bounds.

Any attempts at speech that is outside of the elitist's opinion will be shouted down, protested against, boycotted, insulted, parsed and twisted into words that can now be demonized. Shouts of raciest, sexist, Nazi, and names even more demeaning are used to disrupt, impede and delegitimize any speech the elitist deems contrary to their superior agenda.

This outburst typically takes place before a single word is uttered, and in reality it is promoted by bigotry and hatred. It is the introduction of the university inspired "safe space" concept being brought to the rest of the population. The news media loves it, what great news to report; a bunch of trained protesters shouting down legitimate attempts at talking to the populous, to our country. But, that cannot be permitted, the elitist must stay in control, it is not about their concern for the country, it is a concern about promoting their own ego. *All done at the country's expense.*

Over the past years the populous of this country have lost their voice, they have been minimized as ignorant or just plain stupid. They are not permitted to bring forward their concerns on the direction this country has been taking, with the elitist personality at the forefront of this effort to diminish their relevance.

Major population centers somehow feel they should run the entire country, and done so with an elitist arrogance of being. The self-centered elitist only knows one thing, that they know everything; what is right, what is wrong, and they cannot come to grips with the fact that everyone else does not see and understand how right and how superior they are.

Now, let us keep in mind, no one has, at any point, stood up and proclaimed they want to destroy this country, in fact it is well to the contrary. The only thing that is required is the ego driven elitist's ability to maintain control, this is what causes the conflict. It is not hard to identify the motivation, it is not policy, nor anything to do with reality, but it is the ability to maintain the narrative through domination. The elitist is not interested in compromise; their superiority would never allow any form of open discussion.

The elitist will hold the country hostage while pursuing their opinioned need to stay in the vanguard of the major population centers that have been so well nurtured in the art of bigotry and hatred for any opposing opinion. And, that in itself is fascinating on how they will rail against opinions, which they themselves have supported, but let those same concepts come from the opposition, and they will be demonized. The hypocrisy of the elitist mindset is amazing.

I-10

Hypocrisy

WE HAVE DISCUSSED to some degree the hypocritical aspect of the elitist. They display this on an ongoing basis, with no mention of this disturbing conduct by the news media in general. The facts proving this hypocritical conduct are quite readily found with little effort. No bias needs to be applied to see the facts, it is there for all to see. But, somehow the news media cannot bring themselves to report on these facts, although they will if hypocrisy is displayed by the elitist's antagonists, the ones who do not fit the media's ideologically single minded approach to news reporting.

As we discussed earlier the elitist is not overly concerned about the general welfare of the country; jobs, security, racial and cultural division, the general welfare of the populous is rarely addressed, and if it is, there is *never* any improvement. Their real issues are much more global in scope, more of an altruistic display in nature. Typically these are issues that this country alone cannot resolve, thus elevating the elitist to being seen as a true champion and actually awarded for problems that remain unresolved, and they have done little or nothing to change it. Meanwhile our country corrodes, while the elitist chases the accolades.

They have an answer for everything, but know nothing on how to legitimately improve anything. Policies are only valid if it comes from the elitist's mouth, while the same words from anyone else's lips will be dismissed, and most likely ridiculed. If you take a little time to investigate, you can find that virtually any policy, issue, or action taken by the opposition to the elitist regime was and will be demonized; meanwhile you will discover it duplicates the activities of the elitist. The difference; one gets reported on, while the other does not. *Hypocrisy at its very best...*

I - 1 1

Manipulation

THE ELITIST IS masterful at the manipulation of their dedicated believers and followers. They have an arsenal of well-crafted tools which can be easily utilized, giving their supporters ammunition to demonize any and all who oppose their ideologically motivated theories.

The promotion of political correctness has grown considerably over the past decade, aimed solely at providing a make believe platform that can be easily exploited. Political correctness is used as a form of manipulation to disparage the opposition, and placate the believers.

The most popular politically incorrect subject to introduce is racism; the elitist will throw that term about with no problem. If any opposition is offered, regardless of policy or action, the term racist is used with great effectiveness. The news media loves it, and will follow every accusation of racism as if it were factual. The term racist has become the rally cry of those bigoted individuals who care nothing about the damage it does to our cultural relationships, and said while they openly support actual racist activities taking place that promote division and hatred.

Sadly, those most affected by racism are the real victims of such commentary, meanwhile the elitists garner their support as the true champions of their issues, and yet nothing ever changes. If only the media could provide the truth that is buried in factual history.

History holds the realities to many of the politically correct/incorrect issues of today. Realities that now through manipulation of history have been perverted and twisted to fit the elitist's need to stay in power, using complete denial of their participation in racist issues. Many supposed well informed, well-educated intellectuals seem to have little knowledge of historical fact.

History through the eyes of a cloistered academic ideology and supported by the self-serving news media has lost relevance, and turned into manufactured politically incorrect accusations. The elitist is not stupid, and they are the masters of changing the narrative.

By the way, if my comments should inspire you to investigate historical fact dealing with any aspects of racism, I highly recommend you do it sooner rather than later. The elitist is busy manipulating and altering essential facts through the parsing of real data, and/or complete elimination of what took place in our not so distant past.

Sexism is another well used politically incorrect accusation and thrown about with no regard for authenticity. Once the accusation is made the media picks up on it as a news story, while it is nothing more than an allegation voiced by the elitist wanting to demonize their detractors. Meanwhile the followers believe every word, parroting it over and over until somehow it finds authenticity.

"Nazi" is an often used term by the elitist to garner attention, that is always a winner with the media and of course the supposed informed follower. The nonsense factor that should be applied to such ridiculous, childish commentary is somehow acceptable. To the elitist and their followers this accusation is *not* politically incorrect. In fact, virtually anything that comes from the elitist mouth, regardless on how asinine the narrative, will be applauded by the ideological challenged. They will never see the hypocrisy of their own behavior.

Politically incorrect words and actions are virtually always developed in a closed and exclusionary environment, with the motivation to once again demonize the dissenting opposition to the elitist's ideology. Our culture is being programmed to be afraid of words. Yes, there can be words that are hurtful and demeaning, but this growing censorship of words and opinions are not far away from book burning. No one should be limited by an elitist's concept of what is proper to say, or not to say.

Whether this arbitrary hypothesis of what is right or wrong comes from academia, the news media, some entertainer, or most importantly from our government, free speech should never be limited. This current atmosphere of shutting out differing opinions and ideologies is so contrary to what made this country great, which quite simply is freedom from oppression.

It is unimaginable to me what would take place if the elitist's concept of what they see as acceptable conduct as it relates to open and free speech was applied to them. They would certainly cry foul, and once again the true hypocrisy of elitism would be exposed. They live in a private world, with only their ideology and opinions being valid, all others being politically incorrect, and should be censored and certainly never be heard.

I-12

Survival

SO, IT ALL sounds pretty bleak... How do we survive, those who find themselves as the target of this onslaught of the ideologically superior beings? People who are so assured that their opinions and beliefs are so correct that they are willing to set aside the needs of the country just to perpetuate their own opinionated agenda are certainly troublesome at best, and perilous at worse.

My first reaction to what has been taking place in our country, in today's world, is anger and frustration. The elitist survives in a bubble of support that is provided by the intolerant bigots who see themselves as being inclusive, but with no idea of what that means. From academia, to the media, to our politicians, their hypocrisy is overwhelming; with no idea what damage they are doing to this country. These are powerful people, and they are a true danger to a free and open society; to democracy itself.

So, one must take our anger and frustration and apply it where we can. Obviously, the ballot box is one of the only genuine avenues that the *populous* has in taking the country back from the elitist ideologue. This country cannot help anyone, nor confront any issue until we internally improve ourselves. While the elitist and their followers seek to delegitimize and demonize their opposition they block the country from moving forward, and our ability to legitimately repair this horrendous division that has developed over the past decade, and what we currently suffer from today. Driving a wedge into a country is a concept that has been well defined by our present day elitists, and in past history successfully practiced by many dictators. The separation they seek is a necessity for their survival, and not the country's.

Now, we are off to cast our vote, to alleviate ourselves from the ideologically motivated regulatory overreach of oppressive governance. And, by some phenomenon, our vote wins out, and it appears there is light in the political tunnel! Reform from failed policies and opinions, with a true possibility in repairing the chasm that was so meticulously formed by the self-centered ego-centric elitists may be a possibility.

Sadly, as we have discussed, the elitist does not take defeat well, and even when out of power they seek to undermine and destroy the will of the populous, and done with no regard for the destruction they are imposing on this country.

Their exclusionary tactics affects millions of Americans, promoting hate and division. The one thing that will not get in their way are the facts, and coupled with their use of political theater, spin and demonization, those who subscribe are enamored with such behavior, rushing to support any attack, and with little idea of the damage that is being done.

They do not care, it is their way or the highway, the fact that they are selling out the country is the farthest from their mind, and performed all in the name of their self-indulgent ideology.

The general populous, who has suffered under the elitist's regime, now must suffer again through their thoughtless, mean-spirited attacks, which does nothing for this country. Those in the elitist bubble applaud this conduct. Academia, news media, and the all-knowing entertainment community rally to support any and all attacks on not just those who are now in power, but those who put the opposition there; the forgotten populous.

They have no concern for those who must go off to work every day, who are trying to make a decent life for themselves and their family. They dominate the ones with no voice; with no time to protest, or to rally around the core beliefs that make this arguably one of the greatest countries in the world.

The elitist has no problem in insulting one's values and diminishing the needs of millions, and done by making fun of them, or calling them deplorable names, which somehow bolsters their superiority.

They diminish their opponents character by demonizing the behavior which does not align with their own ideological sensibilities. They are certainly treacherous individuals, with little ability to understand the countries needs, let alone supporting them.

Their feedback comes solely from their protective bubble of existence, failing to comprehend a reality they barely know exists. The news media, in general, will never admit their fallibility; they are so far above the populous, they will never truly be able to understand. The battle, sadly, rages on.

Academia has for years burrowed down into the deepest levels of narcissistic, self-important conduct. With minimal real contact with the outside world, they live in their closed environment, living in their bubble of existence. They will continue to promote close-minded, selective thought, with an exclusionary image they see as intellectually defendable.

The day may come when we can all share the same vision; one of prosperity, safety, and respect for all. Unfortunately, the world is far from that reality, and this country, most certainly, has slid backwards in its attempt to find that civilized existence. With elitists either in control or battling to regain it, we will stagnate as a country; wrapped in some ideological concept that has nothing to do with rescuing this country from decay.

Their goal is to hold on to power, and for that to happen they must form a coalition, starting with the disenfranchised as a captive group of continued supporters who are living on promises that are never fulfilled. They will actively seek to add to this group of disenfranchised, and not to help them, but to add to their constituency.

The next group is the supposed intellectual, these folks who do not live in the same world as we do. They are typically privileged, either by position or wealth, and in many cases suffering from guilt. They see themselves as caring, concerned individuals, but with no real notion on how to implement change.

They see the rest of us as being below them, and totally convinced that they are the only ones with the answers. In reality most are just aligning themselves with the intellectually perceived power elite, and believing whatever is said by those expounding the same ideological rhetoric. They outwardly display concern to help and support the ever growing number of the disenfranchised, while in reality they want to expand their ever growing constituency.

The charismatic, well-spoken and very likeable politician may not be anything more than an empty suited elitist. We put people in office to improve this country... Ask yourself, has this country improved over the past decade? What has the status quo of our political landscape done to provide jobs and security to our citizens? Has education improved? Have answers to our failing entitlement programs been found? Have the real threats to our country been actively addressed? Has the racial and cultural divide improved? Do you honestly have the confidence that everything was being done to keep this country going in the right direction?

Year after year, the country continues to erode, yet we keep putting the same professional politicians in office, filled with promises that never come true.

We need change, we need to stop looking to the uber-ego elitist politician for answers they just do not have. The country right now is being filled with bias, hatred and deception, all in an attempt to keep an elitist group in power.

Stop being manipulated! You have been programmed over time by your environmental upbringing, a biased academic community, a biased news media, an unnatural infatuation with the entertainment industry, or your innate ability to accurately identify the reality around is letting you down.

If you find yourself hating someone that you see as opposing your ideologies, or maybe you just do not like their looks, or more importantly you feel superior to those who do not agree with you because they are stupid, then my friend, I would suggest you wake up. Do not run your life on emotion, there are facts all around you, all you have to do is see them.

I-13

Light In The Tunnel

OUR GOOD FRIENDS in the United Kingdom, through Brexit, are in the process of taking their country back from elitists. Those select few, external of this sovereign country, who had deemed themselves superior in their ability to determine the laws, regulations, and cultural issues have been rejected.

I personally believe other European countries, in time, will follow suit. They have their individual cultures, and certainly should be able to plot their own course. This is not to say there cannot be interaction, trust and partnership in this globally changing world, but no country should be presided over by a select few; only the *true* populous can determine how their country should be governed.

We have seen select areas of our country who want to be in charge of the entire nation, doing everything in their power to disrupt. They will, if necessary, bring the country to a complete halt, blocking our ability to move forward. They fail to understand what the United States represents, and the concepts on which it was founded.

A few highly populated urban centers cannot rule the rest of the country, the very thought that they can comes from a particular mindset; the elitist's. They are convinced they know how everyone should live, think and believe.

As mentioned their attack on the country has become monumental in scope. The centralized, incestuous news media is now in a full out assault on virtually every aspect of what this country should be, a country of freedom, prosperity and safety. A country that cares for all of its' citizens, regardless of heritage, and not just a select few. The elitist now find themselves in a battle to regain control, and believe me they will rip this country apart to do it.

Observe the elitist followers; they take actual joy in the failure at the attempts to repair policies and regulations that have created a chasm in our country, which may already be beyond repair. They take great pride in seeing the government crippled by the elitist's obstructionism with no regard to the damage they are causing. But, I do see hope that we will get out from under the elitist's oppression.

The states have specific rights as clearly spelled out in the Constitution, and once true patriots can bring these rights forward we may find our way back to getting out from under the elitist's control.

We are guaranteed, through the Constitution, that a handful of states cannot over take our government. The elitist can insult, demean and demonize the populous of a majority of states, but it will only fortify the resolve of the majority of the states to take back the country from the elitist domination. The media has been busy making themselves look ridiculous in how they cover and manipulate the news. The universities are now being exposed for the sheltered elitists they are by failing to permit free and open speech, the very Constitutional right they should be promoting and defending.

Yes, there is light in the tunnel, and let's hope that those followers of elitists realize how they have been used and manipulated by those who just seek power and control. Any reasonable person must at one point ask themselves, have I been so indoctrinated that I actually want our leaders to fail because I don't like them? Have I been influenced to hate them? Hatred is a very destructive emotion, and hatred in the hands of a ideologically motivated group or individual can and probably will be devastating.

Puppets are not all that smart... Ask yourself, how smart are you?

I-14

Who Are We?

SO, WHO ARE we?

Are you reasonable and open enough to listen to someone else's opinions and ideologies? Or, do you ridicule and dismiss the input because it just does not align with your ideological perceptions? More importantly, can you accept a verifiable fact as fact, if it does not support your beliefs, or do you just reject it as false? Do you even try to verify this information?

Do you support the efforts of activist protestors who attempt, and many times succeed in censoring free speech by not permitting people who have nothing more to offer than a different point of view? This is done at the expense of those who would like nothing more than to hear the commentary.

Do you find yourself seeking news media outlets which only reports news that supplies you a "safe space" protecting you from any contrary opinions or facts, and done so based solely on your own rooted beliefs? When listening to these news conduits, can you tell the difference between the reporting of real news, versus opinions being conflated into real news? Do you find yourself insulting and making fun of news media outlets reporting *(factual)* news that does not support your ideological beliefs? Do you ever investigate to see if you are receiving all the relevant news?

Do you support having "safe spaces" in this country that are set aside to protect like-minded individuals from hearing anything that they do not agree with? Do you think that pro- tecting a pampered delicate ideology from free speech and open thought is a good idea?

Can you accept the loss of your candidate in an election, and have the ability to understand that this took place based on the decision of millions of other American citizens? Have you taken the stance that no matter what, you cannot support this country in that conclusion?

Give some thought to the above questions. Can you realisti- cally admit to yourself that in many cases your answers are motivated more by bigotry and hate, rather than the reality of what is actually taking place? If so, think about how you are perceived by those that want this country to succeed and to be open to all citizens, and not just supporting the ideological elitist who so desperately wants to be in control. Let me as- sure you, you are not favorably viewed by millions with any real respect.

Can sincerely state that you are content with the country's financial situation, true employment statistics, societal condi- tion and the overall direction this country has taken over the past decade? Do you believe the country is on the right track? Well, I guess the strength of your ideologies and innate ratio- nale to comprehend life around you is serving you very well. *Good luck...*

I must admit, I would be hard pressed to even start to agree with you, but I can, at least, respect you for maintaining your beliefs. Personally, I tend believe that biases and bigoted viewpoints have clouded the capacity to rationally care about anything other than personal opinions. Protecting these opinions through denial, formulated by using little consideration for anything other than one's own selfishness certainly does not move this country forward.

Your innate need to always be right is letting you down. *No one is always right!* When you reject any narrative prior to knowing all the facts and details, coming from a source that you have been programmed and manipulated to hate and demonize; does it supply you with a sense of superiority?

What do we want? Well, I obviously can only speak for myself, although I am confident millions of others agree:

I would like to see the end to the perpetuation of putting this country internally at odds with each other. Continued fanning of the flames to keep racism in the forefront by the elitist leaders who want nothing more than to remain in control of those they contend to care about must be recognized and stopped. Frankly, things should be improving, and not deteriorating. But, with the constant victimizing of an entire race of people just to enable a handful of elitists to remain in their position of domination and control is so obvious, and yet ignored by the elitist media. Do these leaders really care, are they in fact providing assistance? Why are so many ongoing horrific issues taking place in many of our communities, yet totally ignored, while other less concerns are played upon and used to promote divisiveness and division in the country?

I would like to see this country get back to work. There is no reason this should not have been addressed years ago. Jobs should be plentiful! We are a country of consumers; buying products and services at a record pace, yet millions are out of work. We have a population of approximately 325 million, with an employment-to-population percentage of (as of 2013) 67.4%. From 2000 to 2008, we remained in the mid to low 70's%; then dramatically falling by 3% in 2009 and remaining there ever since.

I would like the security and safety of this country to return to what it once was. We have lost the credibility as a strong caring country. We have set upon a course to demonize our own country; imploding from within; apologizing for being a successful culture; surrendering to those who want to see this country fail. Sadly, much of this philosophy comes from within. Who knows, the time might even come when the elitist population centers will attempt to secede from the United States!

I would like to see those self-important elitists who are continually at odds with everything that doesn't fit their self-indulgent ideologies and opinions understand they are not that relevant in the big scheme of things, although we all know they want to be. Look, I am not making them out to be bad people, but they do tend see themselves as all-knowing and certainly being intellectually above the rest of us. That does not make for a healthy leadership.

Paying lip service to issues has nothing to do with addressing the realities that are taking place in this country today. Throwing stones at efforts to put this country back together just because it is being done by those you just happen to hate, falls far short of caring for the entire country, and not just based on their own limited view of right and wrong. They are not the rulers of this country, although it is quite obvious they genuinely believe they are.

I would like to see the ongoing need for a majority of the elitist media wanting to apply their ideologies to what should be factual news, and pushing their own obvious biases to diminish and demonize millions of Americans to come to an end! They are banking on what they see as our ignorance, they know they are in power, and they would love to be in a position to socially engineer virtually all aspects of this country.

Who are we? Do we care about this country? I doubt the average, hardworking American sees this country as anything else but a country of freedoms, and certainly not a country that is socially and culturally controlled and directed by the government.

Our country has been diminished in the eyes of the global community, and it is no surprise to see that many countries are pleased to see it. Yes, we are, or at least once was, a powerful country, but as the elitists within the elite positions of power took control, they wasted no time in taking the opportunity to manipulate the narrative to fit their perception of what this country should be. Sadly, their vision has left us appearing weak, and permitting in many cases the jealousies and resentments harbored by other countries to surface. The world community piled on, and we just kept on bowing to those looking to pull us apart.

I defy anyone to point out when the United States has acted in any way that did not support and defend those who were not able to defend themselves from attack. We have gone to war and lost more American lives, more than I even want to mention, all in the defense of other countries. That includes countries with cultures far divorced from our own, yet we cared and died in their defense.

We annually supply billions of dollars to those countries which have come to us for financial aid, with many of those dollars doing nothing more than lining the pockets of the leaders of those countries, yet we continue. I doubt we do this because we are a selfish, uncaring country. Yet, when we try to simply maintain our own sovereign rights by following our own laws we are called exclusionary.

Patriotism has been under attack for some years now, mostly coming from the news media and academia, and seemly supported, to some degree, by our leaders. Yes, I have noticed that certain aspects of our government have gone out of their way to support this now ongoing undermining of what this country once represented and stood for; their judgment in doing so escapes me. It is something that I am apparently too ignorant to understand, and why it would be done. I do know one thing, it all comes from those who are absolutely sure they know better.

Regardless of your political affiliation, ask yourself what is more important, your country or supporting those who are playing on your ideological beliefs. What do they want? To stay in, or gain, control!

How does the politician earn a living? By being a politician of course. That's their job. You would think they would want to do what is the best for this country. They certainly talk about it a lot, yet the real issues never seem to improve, and in many cases continue to deteriorate. It almost looks like their main concern is not bettering life for any of us, but rather hanging on to their entrenched ideological base, and when the opportunity arises add to that constituency.

The elitist has goals; to be in an elite position, and most importantly to be in control. One thing that must be understood: you do not mess with the elitist's ego...

II: Surviving Elitism

The Vote

II-15

The Right

LET US REVIEW one of our most significant aspects of living in a republic; our ability to choose the governmental leaders of this country. A right, which is being usurped by the elitist power base.

With the power-elite now controlling so many aspects of our virtual mainstream society, they can manipulate realities through censorship, exclusionary rhetoric, and by playing on those who are easily managed, or those so entrenched in an ideological belief where common sense and intellect are set aside.

The fundamental right to vote, or at least who are eligible to vote, was not originally defined in the Constitution of the United States. It was initially set to allow each State to determine who was eligible. Only through future Amendments to the Constitution was the right to vote more clearly defined.

The 15th Amendment, Section 1: "The right of the citizens of the United States to vote shall not be denied or abridged by the United States or by any State on account of race, color, or previous condition of servitude."

The 19th Amendment to the Constitution of the United States: "The right of all citizens of the United States to vote shall not be denied or abridged by the United States or by any State on account of sex."

Now, although these two Amendments do make specific determinations as to race, color, previous condition of servitude and sex, they certainly insure the fundamental right to vote for all. This assurance of voting rights extends to all citizens regardless of any consideration given to their comprehension and understanding of the issues, or knowledge of the candidates that are running for office.

II-16

The Candidates

WE HAVE, OR certainly should have, learned throughout our political history that those running for office are not necessarily being honest with their positions or abilities to function in the office for which they aspire to hold. More often than not, it appears apparent that ego, elitism and their individual ideology is at the forefront of their desire to be in office, and this is true at any level of sought after governmental positions. This is not to say there are those who are not committed and quite genuine in their pursuit of serving the public good, but so often we find that they are few and far between.

In reality we must face certain aspects of the personality of those running for office. The first is ego, without an ego motivating their aspirations there would be few putting themselves into the political arena. This in itself is not concerning. For better or worse a varied level of ego is a part of us all, and generally is the inspirational drive to put them in the race.

The second is the elitist personality; they believe they know better, and in many cases feel they are well above the hoi polloi in which they will be representing. This is, and should be, very concerning. Just because you think you know better is in no way an indication that in fact you do.

The third, and probably the most dangerous, is their individual ideology. Obviously, we all have and support some form of ideology. The reality: Ideology, or what we believe, has little to do with fact. Whether your political bent is left or right, the current ideology of either political party certainly does not seek the decline or cause collapse of the United States. No politician stands in front of the electorate and pontificates on how they will make things worse in our country, but you will hear ad infinitum on how their opponent will be doing just that very thing.

Politicians play on your ideology; they will say whatever is needed to pit you against their opponent, and the party of their opponent. Some parties specialize in name calling, and for those supporting the same political ideology they love it. Comedy shows in many cases have become the new source for news, and why not? They make fun of all the things that support your beliefs; it may be great fun, but sadly has nothing to do with what may or may not be reality. Comedians as political pundits, what a great concept! Based on their political ideology, and playing to a particular audience, they reinforce beliefs, which now become pseudo fact to their willing and easily manipulated listeners.

II-17

Ideology

THIS IS A word that you have, and will continue to read throughout this writing. Ultimately, it is at the core of most problems with the individual vote in our country. So, before we proceed let's make sure we fully understand the meaning of the word:

ideology:

"The body of ideas reflecting the social needs and aspirations of an individual, a group, a class, or culture. A set of doctrines or beliefs that form the basis of political, economic, or other system."

For most of us our ideologies are formed, or begin to be formed, at a very early age. Various factors will help form these beliefs: Our environment, our parents, our associations, but most importantly our inherent innate abilities; an understanding that is produced by the ability of the mind, rather than absorbed through experience, as in *an innate knowledge of right and wrong.*

There is a saying "We don't know what we don't know". It has a complexity that escapes many. For example "I know, I do not know how to play the violin" so that proves I know what I don't know. But, how can you possibly know something that you are totally unaware of? You do not know what you do not know. I go through this silliness to highlight a point, ignorance can be found in the ideologically motivated individual or group holding preconceived points of view without knowing all the relevant facts, *not knowing, what they do not know.*

Supporting any point of view based solely on ideology, and to such a degree in which reality and facts are disregarded in exclusive support of your beliefs, on the surface, certainly seems to display a level of ignorance.

Now, let's make sure we understand my use of the word ignorance; it is used only to describe the lacking of education, knowledge, or being unaware, or uniformed on any particular subject. Do not confuse ignorance with stupidity. I do not believe any individual's ideology is stupid, regardless of its content. I support and welcome anyone's beliefs/ideologies, but whether one likes it or not, many of us support ideologies that are not fact or reality based, and far from the truth that surrounds us. All of this is being said within the realm of politics only, and please, do not equate any of my comments to religious or spiritual beliefs.

II-18

The Media And Ideology

FIRST LET US separate news from opinions. These two aspects of the *news* media have become a blurred line of reporting. Biased news reporting has for the most part become common place. Ideology has dramatically infiltrated the news, and the journalists reporting it, whether in print or on-air reporting.

The most popular method of this is through omission of real news that should be reported. It does not take much investigating, but it is astounding on how much news, *real* news, goes unreported because it does not fit, nor support the ideology of the media outlet. It has become so prevalent and so well executed, that when other competing outlets do report it, it is seen as insignificant at best, and a lie at worst. This happens so often that it has now become an accepted reality of news journalism.

Now, this is not to say that any news media outlet cannot have an opinion or ideology to expound upon. Certainly they are welcome to do so; this will attract those whose ideology agrees with their opinions being expressed. This can be supported through editorials and op-ed pieces that are not represented as news reporting. But, selective news reporting; not reporting all the available news just to placate their subscribers is certainly a journalistic failure, and a true disservice to what should be a fully informed public, regardless of ideology.

The unbiased reporting of who, what, when and where must be considered a reliable source of news. Does your news source give you all the news, or just what you want to hear? Do not let your ideology get in the way of hearing it all. It would be like schools teaching our children just facts that support a certain ideology and point of view. That would border on being criminal! *But, that could never happen...*

Know the difference between opinion and real news; listening to other's opinions can be informative, and in today's world an absolute must. But, be sure it is not a discussion centering on childish attempts at manipulating you through name calling or selective facts by the parsing of words and spinning reality into fantasy to fulfill your ideological beliefs. One thing to be very aware of, if you are viewing an opinion panel *(talking heads)* and they are discussing an issue that has not been reported as a news item on that particular network; please, change the channel.

Do you have a single source of news? Does your news source always report just what you want to hear? Most importantly, can you accept *facts* that are contrary to your ideological beliefs as legitimate and relative?

II-19

The Electorate

THE UNITED STATES has a two party system; we do have the outliers, but they will typically caucus with one of the two parties. The electorate in this country tends to align with one of these two parties, but thankfully we do have the independent voter. For the most part they tend to be more informed, more involved in the decision by paying attention to the facts, or at least their perception of the facts, and they ultimately are the deciders of most elections.

Those who are on the devout left believe anything and everything that the left has to say. It doesn't matter what the reality may be, they will always vote to the left, they will demean, ridicule and discredit anyone even slightly leaning to the ideological right. They only hear what they what to hear, and disregard anything that even mildly disturbs their beliefs. Their voter base is unshakable, no matter what; they do not need to be informed because information and facts contrary to their beliefs will not change their vote.

Now, before those who fit the above description head's explode, the same exact thing can be said for those on the devout right. They are what they are, for them the vote is simple.

II-20

Right & Wrong

WHO IS RIGHT, who is wrong? Like we discussed earlier, no politician touts hurting or destroying this country, they all talk of making things better, fixing the problems and the woes of this country. One side wants to do it one way, while the other takes a different path, all aiming for the same outcome.

What do we the people want: Freedom, peace, prosperity for all? Probably that's what the majority desires. So, it is a relatively simple list, and on the surface it seems like it should be a relatively easy list to satisfy. Who would be against freedom, peace and prosperity? Apparently we are; *we the people*.

We have a document that is genius in its simplicity, a map to that simple list of wants which benefits us all. The Constitution with its' Amendments plainly spells out the path to those goals, yet year after year, election after election, things seem to decay.

Throughout the years, during the rarest of times there were glimmers of achieving what I would like to believe we all want to find in life. But, without fail, the opposing political party will disparage those times, because it is a direct threat to their existence, and their very power. We the people were manipulated by that opposing party, which played to our ide-ologies; we rejected whatever successes that may have made just to support a charming, well-spoken elitist politician.

The ego driven elitist, those supposed intellectuals of our so-ciety, along with greed and corruption, whether in or out of power, now dominates our political landscape. Those who seek power to salve their own ideologies and egos strive to stay in control, using any means necessary.

Sadly, it would not take that much effort to investigate who we have put into these positions of power. Even if they meant to do the very best for this country they were not equipped to do so. They carried ideologies that are flawed, even though well meaning, and as they moved forward with their con-cepts, those who supported them refused to see the mistakes that were quite apparent. An ideology formed at the youngest of age, and lacking the necessary wisdom, now determines the most important of decisions, and the future of this country.

We see other countries, who have embraced other psycholog-ical and political methods who contend to pursue the same life that we seek, but there are no real successes.

So, who is right? In reality it is probably a mix of both ide-ologies, blended by reason and logic, and certainly *without* political gamesmanship. But, for sure, it is not those with egos so large they cannot admit to a mistake or failure. The elitist will stay the course directly in the face of failure, while the ability to change and alter direction, when needed, is dis-played by their opposition, it is seen as chaotic incompetence.

It is the elitist who will tell you what to do and how to live, while they live by a completely different set of rules, they are superior, and know better. The regulators are in power. Government positions, at virtually all levels, are far too lucrative, financially, in authority and power. *Mr. Smith has not gone to Washington!* And, has not for some years...

II-21

The Uninformed

THE WELL INFORMED voter; in today's world, is pretty much of an oxymoron. As we have discussed ideology is now, and has been, all the information most voters use. If you're on the left you do not need any more information than what the left tells you, and the same for the folks on the right. The left and right throw insults back and forth, bringing up issue after issue of how the other side has lied, cheated and mislead the public, and for the most part they are both right. But, who cares; so my candidate lied through their teeth, deceived and got caught at it, so what. Listen they could drop kick a baby, but I would vote for them anyway. *It just doesn't matter...*

As far as issues go, the political parties' best bet is to hang their hat on some topic that is not directly addressable or solvable. Then go forth by railing about that issue and blaming virtually everything that happens on it. Those who subscribe to that parties' ideology jump aboard, take on a superior elitist stance, giving them a reason to throw stones at the other side. It's not that we are all simple minded, but we do tend to be very easily led. What the heck, no thought or investigation has to be done; my side said so; it must be true.

There are those in our society that have proven their success in other fields. They are decision makers, intelligent with the ability to lead, and most importantly willing to make a decision. They may not fit the typical mold of a politician and not having the political savvy that we have come to expect, which is probably constructive. For the most part these folks steer clear of entering the political arena, but when they do, for the most part they are rejected in favor of the experienced politician.

Of course we should pick the experienced politician, they have this wonderful track record of knowing how to get elect- ed, probably because they are charming or good speakers, or better yet nice looking.

How about those achievements!

Well, maybe not so much, but that is who we get to vote for. We do not need to be informed to vote for these professional politicians, who for the most part have been on the public's teat for most of their adult life. Do we need an elected official who has found political success by being able to survive in the glad-handing, lobbyist ridden, self-serving world of politics? *Apparently!*

I I - 22

We The People

WE THE PEOPLE... I see it as simple straight forward statement that proudly opens the Constitution of the United States of America. We the citizens of this country have gathered to-gether to promote the betterment and welfare for all. In fact let us revisit that opening paragraph:

"We the People **of the United States, in Order to form a more perfect Union, establish Justice, insure domestic Tranquility, provide for the common defence, promote the general Welfare, and secure the Blessings of Liberty to ourselves and our Prosperity, do ordain and establish this Constitution for the United States of America."**

Now, if you take a moment to read the Constitution and its' Amendments you will find that it delineates and promotes every aspect of our freedoms and rights that this country has been founded upon.

Somehow the pride in our country, in our freedoms, that have been so eloquently stated in the Constitution, are now being eroded by, guess who; *we the people*. Of all the words which have now become so incredibly powerful; the "politically in-correct" words now seem to have a force that can inflect pain to such a degree that they cannot even be uttered; a level of sensitivity so acute that the mere whisper of these words can inspire a riot. Yet, the words that describe the desires and hopes of our country's founders, which were written for the future of this country, and not for their own political betterment, are now somehow minimized, if not completely over looked.

In recent decades the Constitution has been under attack. These attacks are basically justified by wanting special privilege attached to special interests. To offer changes and/or Amendments to the Constitution that in effect takes the rights away from one to satisfy another the rights of all will then be lost. Keep in mind the Constitution and its' Amendments includes all citizens of this country.

Under the Constitution you are welcome to and encouraged to pursue and enjoy all the rights that this country affords you. But, there is one exception; you are not welcome to rights which take the rights of others away.

So, why do I blame us, "we the people?" Because we are the ones who stopped caring, we let others, through their tailored to please constituency focused comments, promises, spins and lies, to speak for us. That may be okay, but if those "others" are only pursuing their egotistical elitist needs with little interest in the people who they will be representing, well now we are in trouble. And, frankly, we are in trouble.

Our politicians and the political parties they represent have lost sight of the flag, and the brilliant goal so well spelled out in the Constitution. They set out to facilitate a platform that sets them apart from the other party, they manufacture issues and opposing views that somehow only they can champion. They must diminish and demonize the rival party and candidates, and we the people, applaud and support these efforts. We must, it's our party, and right or wrong they align with our ideology.

During numerous casual interviews I have asked various individuals about their ideologies. I do not, or at least try not, to comment on their views, and I for the most part just listen. It is amazing how often they express views, yet live lifestyles that are contrary to their own political beliefs. They may be well to the left, yet conduct their lives with many conservative behaviors. And, the same can be said for those from the far right, behaving in a rather liberal fashion. Now, on those rare occasions when I mention this conundrum of their philosophy versus lifestyle actions, I am typically greeted with a level of irritation or even anger. How dare their beliefs be questioned, even though it is their very own words that are being played back against their own ideology!

The word hypocrite comes to mind, but that seems cruel and certainly demeaning. I understand their beliefs, but I fail to understand how you can defend and believe in one thing, yet live and conduct yourself in the opposing fashion.

During these casual conversations I will often mention various Presidents, from either party, depending upon my knowledge of where their particular political leaning is. The most often used word that comes up, whether talking about a President from the left or from the right; both current and from history, is "hate." They hate that President! Of course, it all depends upon where their political ideology lies. But, when asked why, more often than not, they really do not have a specific answer; typically if they do, it is some insignificant and usually trumped up reason that has little to do with reality, fact, or history. But, for the most part I hear, "I don't know, I just don't like them!"

Most folks seem uninformed and rely solely on some "talking head's" opinion that has been thoroughly manipulated to support their own beliefs. In fact, it is remarkable how often the supposed knowledgeable political expert that is quoted is a comedian as the source for their views.

I've been pretty hard on ideologies. I have made it sound as though all ideologies are inconsequential, forgive me, because they certainly are not. But, if you find yourself automatically throwing stones at those with opposing views without any true investigation and without knowing all the facts, what validity does your opinion have?

Opinions should not solely be formed on parsed statements, opinion editorials, and certainly not on political spin, but rather real facts, based on *all* the available resources, and certainly not just information and opinions from sources that support your life long ideologies and points of view. Then pursue your ideology, but do it with an informed honesty, not one that you are manipulated into by an ego driven elitist politician. If they lied once, they will lie again.

We, the citizens of the United States, live in what is called a republic. Now, I know everyone reading this knows what that means, but if you would permit me, I would like to restate its' meaning, if for nothing more than my own benefit:

republic:

"A political order whose head of state is not a monarch, and in modern time is usually a president. A nation that has such a political order. A political order in which the supreme power lies in a body of citizens who are entitled to vote for officers and representatives responsible to them. A nation that has such a political order."

It is basic to our existence in this country. We the people have the supreme power to vote in or out of office our officers and representatives; that is our political order. So, if that is true who would be at fault if the country is not functioning in a way that is providing freedom, peace and prosperity for all? **We the people!**

The vote is everything and, a vote without understanding the facts and realities of what and who you are voting for, and based solely on an ideology is a misguided vote at best, but more likely a vote that is damaging to our very well being. Do you know specifically about who you are voting for? Have listened to and discovered information that is fact, and not just the facts that support your ideology? Have you taken into account the essentials that are directly contrary to your ideologies, and then balance those facts, fully knowing who you are putting into office? Then you are an informed voter, and your informed vote is truly supporting the republic.

————◆▶——————◀◆————

III: SURVIVING ELITISM

The Elitist's Guide to Understanding the Electoral College

————◆▶——————◀◆————

Note: *This article is not intended to support any political party, nor is it a commentary on the outcome of the 2016 Presidential election. It does however use that election period as an example of the workings of the Electoral College, and why Article II of the Constitution is in place to protect the election process from political manipulation.*

III-23

Political Manipulation

WHEN THE LOSER of the Presidential election receives more of the popular vote than the Electoral Presidential winner, there are always those who will criticize the election process. These individuals now believe *(due to their loss)* that the system has failed and should be changed.

They contend to not understand the genius of the Electoral College, and the true benefit it brings to the United States of America. The very name of this country should give you the answer; the "***United States***." Each State carries, regardless of population, the equal and balanced right to determine the leader of the executive branch of the country. This is evident in the Constitution, which prescribes that the Senate be composed of two Senators from each State, regardless of size and population.

The Electoral College provides less populous states some additional leverage to preserve the presidency independent of Congress, and generally to insulate the election process from political manipulation. Each State is an *equal* member of the United States.

III-24

Simple Example

AN EASY WAY to understand the Electoral concept is to use the example of living in a condominium:

Each unit has joint and equal rule over the entirety of the shared condominium complex. When the governing board and/or issues of the condo are voted upon, each unit gets one vote, with the majority of the unit votes deciding the winner or decision outcome. It is irrelevant on how many individuals live in any particular unit. *One unit; one vote...*

Now, if there were a handful of units which were highly populated; so populated that just a few units could literally outweigh the population balance of the total complex, the entire condominium community would be dominated by just a few units.

It would not matter what the issue was, or whether they were correct in their opinions, they would dominate the entire complex!

Decisions would then be made based solely on the lifestyle within a highly populated, and quite possibly over populated, handful of units. They would not represent the average unit owner, nor care about their issues or needs. They live within the insulated bubble of their unit, and care more about their needs and opinions then that of the needs and opinions of the majority of other unit owners.

III-25

The Consequences

WE CANNOT, AS a united country, permit a few highly populated counties to determine the governance of the entire Federal Government. Each state by popular majority vote determines how that state will apply the number of Electoral votes to be counted.

In the 2016 election, Trump won 30 States, for a total of 306 Electoral votes; while Clinton won 20 States, and 232 Electoral votes. According to the Associated Press, Clinton won 487 counties nationwide, compared with 2,626 for Trump.

Clinton won the total popular vote by **2.9** million (2.2 %,) out of 128.8 million total votes. In looking at just California alone, the consequences of merely using the total popular vote alone can easily be demonstrated; Clinton won California by **3.4** million votes.

The factual impact is obvious; if just a handful of counties within the State of California alone were not counted, Trump would have won the total popular vote, which would still include all of the popular votes from New York city, Miami-Dade county Florida, and Cook county in Illinois.

The *majority* of the *United States,* having the shared and equal ownership of this country decided the 2016 election, and not a select group of likeminded individuals residing in California. Literally, just a portion of this one state could dominate every election.

Without the Electoral College the United States would deteriorate into a country dominated by a select group who would cater to and listen to only like-minded individuals, with no regard for the needs and desires of the rest of the country. No country should ever be left to an *exclusive* portion of its population.

The urban center elitist feels assured that they know more than the rest of the country, and yet it is these very population centers that appear, in many cases, to have the most prevailing internal problems, which never realistically seem to get resolved, and most interestingly, rarely reported upon by the news media.

IV: Surviving Elitism

Final Evaluation

Disbelief

IF YOU HAVE managed to get this far in my commentary, I tend to believe you have probably reached an opinion on what you have read.

I know there are those who will not accept that the news media, in general, is so biased that they would censor and manipulate the news to conform to their and your political ideology. To those, I would suggest taking some time to genuinely do some research and not just on some ideologically motivated blog contending to be the news. I am referring to a real examination of what is and was reported by your news source, and what was not, what was described as real news, and what was opinion masquerading as news.

I know there will be those who will challenge the contention that our universities censor free speech, or promote a "safe space" for those individuals who cannot handle commentary that is contrary to what they have been programmed to believe, and must be protected from it. To those who do not believe there are universities that offer credited classes on how to protest and obstruct the current administration, you would be mistaken. Again, do some research, because apparently your news source is letting you down.

I am very confident that there are those who will deny that their political leaders would say and do anything to stay in or regain lost power. Or, refute that a politician would attempt to prove their failures were in fact not failures at all by lying and changing the narrative, and by typically blaming someone else. If so, I am confident you have come to the conclusion that the politicians you support would never be obstructionists, harming this country through those actions.

The legitimacy of these activities are all around you, and while denying reality may work for you intrinsically it does not speak well of your ideological beliefs. If you have to insult, deny, ignore, refute, dismiss, and totally shut down any input that is divergent to your concepts of reality; what does that say about you?

Today our country is in conflict. The flames of this struggle are being well fanned by the elitist mentality, seeking praise and recognition, with dreams of a lasting legacy. But, at what cost? A chasm has been manufactured that has divided this country more so than at other time in modern history. Is that what we want as part of our culture? Personally, I would like to see us work together, but the elitist will never permit that. We must be at odds for them to find a cause for their minions to rally around.

We know who the elite are: the news media, academia, entertainment, and of course our ever trusted politicians. Now, what do those elite positions all have in common? As we have discussed ad nauseam; recognition, adulation, power and control, all feeding their a super egos. Again, please understand, I do not say that all elites are elitists, but it is getting difficult to find those who display a genuine concern for this country, and done so without attempting to socially engineer our culture to fit their ideological vision. Genuine integrity is in short supply, and as the elitists try to maneuver their way to prominence, celebrity and acclaim, they require a base constituency that blindly supports and applauds their narrative.

I guess one can understand how their community of supporters of seemly intelligent individuals can be lead to follow such a personality, they are also in the business of needing the recognition, and vying for accolades. They do not recognize this behavior within themselves because they share the same elitist-ego that props up their personas. Frankly, if I did not find their outrageous performance so irritating, I would probably feel pity for them. *It cannot be easy being them...*

The real victims of this superior ego is the disenfranchised population of this country, those who struggle to find a reasonably decent life in a country that is so rich with freedom and wealth that should easily be enjoyed by all. Yet, year after year, they hear how they will be lifted from poverty and crime, something they endure as a regular part of their daily lives. All they have to do is vote for and support those making that promise; a promise that is never fulfilled, and soon forgotten about. But, when the time is right, the elitist will come for their votes, armed with the same assurances of bettering their existence.

Take the time to investigate and question, and not just from sources that will conciliate your ideology, but with a true and responsible examination of the *facts*.

IV-27

Understanding

FOR THOSE WHO recognize the realities of what the elitist mindset has brought to our society, and the impact of the narcissistic personality that is so self-involved they see nothing more than their own ideology, I know you understand. The evidence is all around us.

You have the ability to look beyond the pettiness, name calling, unabashed hatred, and the incessant need to fabricate politically correct scenarios used for nothing more than to demonize anyone who does not align with their opinionated ideologies.

You have listened to the extremely hateful commentary, ranging from wanting to blow up the Whitehouse, to masked violent protestors attempting to obstruct free speech, to the millions being called deplorable... Actually, the list of the hateful rhetoric would be far too long to even try to display it all. The point is, you know it is happening, and yet you are the one being framed as the bigot, the hater! All you have to do is watch the evening news to see that you are the problem, your very existence is disturbing the elitist's delicate ideology.

I wonder what would happen if under an administration that

is viewed as deplorable and hated, one that is not wrapped up in some lofty altruistic ideology, would legitimately improve our country and our lives, would the elitist and their dedicated followers admit it? What if the chasm that separates our country were to heal? What if jobs returned to this country, bringing a true and growing economy back to our shores? What if the threats and attacks on this country were brought to a close, would it stop the haters from hating? *My opinion, not on a bet!*

Hang in there, my friends. Hope does spring eternal.

www.ingramcontent.com/pod-product-compliance
Lightning Source LLC
Chambersburg PA
CBHW021546290526
45785CB00004BA/1880

* 9 7 8 1 4 7 8 7 8 8 9 6 6 *